CREDIT SCORE REPAIR

*How to Repair Your Credit and Boost Your Score Fast –
Delete Judgments, Inquiries and Negative Accounts*

THE COMPLETE CREDIT REPAIR EDITION

Copyright © 2017, 2019 - by Dana Lee
All Rights Reserved.

Published By:

CyberLearners, LLC.
Cleveland, OH

Table of Contents

Introduction 1

Chapter 1: What Is A Fico Score And How It Is Calculated...............3

Chapter 2: Understanding Your Credit Report And Cerdit Bureaus...........5

Chapter 3: Why You Need A Good Credit Today...9

Chapter 4: How To Get All Your Reports For Free Online 12

Chapter 5: What Affects Your Score The Most 15

Chapter 6: You Have An Unfair Advanatage With The Consumer Laws – Use Them 18

Chapter 7: How The Fair Credit Acts Protect You..21

Chapter 8: Boost Your Score In 1 Day By Opting Out At This Website ...24

Chapter 9: How To Remove Credit Inquiries Fast..25

Chapter 10: How To Remove Negative Items Fast 31

Chapter 11: How To Delete Public Collections And Judgements 38

Chapter 12: Section 609 Credit Repair Method..44

Chapter 13: Fast Credit Repair After Foreclosure...47

Chapter 14: Fast Credit Repair After Medical Judgements 50

Chapter 15: Quick Techniques To Rebuild Credit 53

Chapter 16: How To Get Lender Offers 56

Chapter 17: How To Build Business Credit..59

Chapter 18: Stop Collectors Fast 62

Chapter 19: How To Negotiate And Settle Large Debts 65

Chapter 20: Maintaing Your Credit 68

Chapter 21: Fraud And Identity Theft Prevention 71

Conclusion 77

Legal Disclaimers

This book is not giving any legal advice and we are not attorneys – any examples or strategies written here are the author's personal experience and opinion.

This Book is reproduced below with the goal of providing information that is as accurate and reliable as possible. Regardless, purchasing this Book can be seen as consent to the fact that both the publisher and the author of this book are in no way experts on the topics discussed within and that any recommendations or suggestions that are made herein are for entertainment purposes only. Professionals should be consulted as needed prior to undertaking any of the action endorsed herein.

This declaration is deemed fair and valid by both the American Bar Association and the Committee of Publishers Association and is legally binding throughout the United States.

Furthermore, the transmission, duplication or reproduction of any of the following work including specific information will be considered an illegal act irrespective of if it is done electronically or in print. This extends to creating a secondary or tertiary copy of the work or a recorded copy and is only allowed with express written consent from the Publisher. All additional right reserved.

The information in the following pages is broadly considered to be a truthful and accurate account of facts and as such any inattention, use or misuse of the information in question by the reader will render any resulting actions solely under their purview.

There are no scenarios in which the publisher or the original author of this work can be in any fashion deemed liable for any hardship or damages that may befall them after undertaking information described herein.

Additionally, the information in the following pages is intended only for informational purposes and should thus be thought of as universal. As befitting its nature, it is presented without assurance regarding its prolonged validity or interim quality. Trademarks that are mentioned are done without written consent and can in no way be considered an endorsement from the trademark holder.

Results by author are personal and are not indicative what the reader will achieve

"The Consumer Credit Laws Are In Favor Of the Debtor – Not the Creditor, But Most Americans Do Not Know This And Allow the Powers-That-Be To Manipulate Their Credit"

Forward by Author:

Who am I am why did I write this book?

In my late 20's I had some financial problems due to poor financial decisions and health problems that ended in several medical bills. This consequently led to a terrible financial storm of public judgments and garnishments that destroyed my credit and depressed my lifestyle for several years because I did not know that I could fight and repair my credit.

My credit turnaround started when; at my lowest point, a friend I worked with gave me a simple book on how to repair my credit using consumer laws. I implemented some of the techniques with my own twists and creativity and achieved a 750 REAL score (the ones lenders see…not the fake ones you buy online) in only 1 year. It took me this long because I had OVER 12 bad accounts and over 5 public judgements, my credit was really bad.

Today my FICO credit score from all major bureaus hovers between 810 and 830 and has been there for a long time.

As a former victim of bad credit, which was as low as 409 FICO at one point, I know all too well what it's like not having good credit:

- Having to deal in cash and money orders.

- Cashing my paychecks at check-checking stores.

- Not being able to rent a decent apartment.

- Rejected for cell phones and carriers.

- Insurance companies turning me down.

- Rejected by car finance companies.

- Potential employers turned me down because my credit was so bad.

When my credit was bad, I had a good government job making $55,000+ a year, but couldn't even get insurance or rent an decent apartment. No one cared how much money or income I had; **it was ALL ABOUT THE CREDIT SCORE. To say this was frustrating is an understatement.**

Unfortunately, this is the American life.

<u>**Without good or fair credit you pay more**</u>, it's a rigged system set up to take advantage of people in certain financial circumstances.

BUT, you are not powerless; there is a flip side to this credit game. Many years ago our government gave us a way to get our credit back and protect it from sharks. But we have to do the work ourselves, and not trust someone else to do it for us.

Roughly 30 percent of all Americans are dealing with a poor credit score and more are falling into the trap of bad credit on a daily basis.

INTRODUCTION

When you are at the bottom of a debt-shaped hole it can appear as though the deck is stacked against you and that you have no way of climbing your way out. This is quite simply not the case and the following chapters will discuss everything you need to know in order to get started on the path to an improved credit rating today.

You will learn about the basics including why you need good credit, what a FICO score is and how it is calculated, the things that affect your score the most and how to get your credit reports (all three of them) for free. You will also learn about the Fair Credit Reporting Act and other consumer protection laws and how they protect you. You will find out how to opt out of unwanted credit inquiries, remove those that are on your credit report and also remove a wide variety of negative items from your credit reports.

From there you will learn all about a variety of credit repair methods regardless of the situation that led to them. You will also how to get multiple offers from lenders, build credit with a small business and how to stop collectors in their tracks and negotiate and settle debts of varying sizes. Finally, you will learn how to maintain good credit and prevent identity theft or fraud from ruining your hard work.

There are plenty of books on this subject on the market, thanks again for choosing this one Every effort was made to ensure it is full of as much useful information as possible and we offer free letter templates and articles on our website.

CHAPTER 1

WHAT IS A FICO SCORE AND HOW IT IS CALCULATED

Your FICO score is a measure of the overall quality of your credit that was developed by the Fair Isaac Corporation which is a software company that focuses on analytics and works with businesses in more than 90 countries around the world. While it is not the only available metric for determining credit score, it is the one that is most commonly used by a wide range of different lenders and companies when it comes to determining the level of risk that is associated with a given individual.

The calculations that go into determining a person's credit score are proprietary which means that the Fair Isaac Company doesn't share them with anyone. However, some of the details regarding it have been found out, including the fact that a FICO score is based on a handful of difference categories of various levels of importance to the total. It has been determined that payment history is weighted with approximately 35 percent relevance, amount owed has a 30 percent relevance, credit history length has a 15 percent relevance, abundance of new credit has a 10 percent relevance and type of credit used has a 10 percent relevance.

Payment history relates to how prompt you have been when it comes to previous payments you have made to various creditors. It also factors in things such as delinquency, number of accounts you have in collections, bankruptcy and how long it has been since these problems appeared on your record. As such, the greater number of problems that you have had in this regard, the worse your overall FICO score is going to be.

When it comes to the amount you current owe to lenders, FICO takes into account the amount of debt you currently have as well as the types of accounts you hold and the number of different accounts that you currently hold. This section also looks at your current financial situation as a whole which means the more debt you currently have the weaker your score will be.

The other areas that FICO looks into are all relatively self-explanatory. Overall, the longer you go without having anything negative added to your credit history, the better your overall FICO score is going to be. It is also important to keep in mind that your FICO score will only take into account information that has been added to your credit report which is not the sum total of information that a lender will look at while determining if you are eligible for a loan or what your rates will be

CHAPTER 2

UNDERSTANDING YOUR CREDIT REPORT AND THE CREDIT BUREAUS

Your credit report is actually more complicated than it may appear at first blush, simply because you are actually dealing with reports from three different agencies, TransUnion, Experian and Equifax. What this means is that you will need to check each of the three reports on a regular basis to ensure you have all the pertinent information on your current credit score.

Anatomy of a credit report

While the three major credit reports are going to vary somewhat, information is always going to be grouped into four major categories, these are credit inquires, creditor information, public record information and personal information.

Personal information: The personal information section is going to include things like you name and any aliases you use, your social security number, date of birth, employment information and your current and previous addresses.

Public record information: This section will include any currently pending legal issues related to your current financial situation.

This can include bankruptcies, wage garnishments, judgements and liens. A TransUnion report will also show the approximate date when these details will be removed from your report.

Creditor information: This section will show all of your debts that have been turned over to a collection agency and all of the lines of credit that you currently have. Additionally, you will find details outlining the status of the account in question, if you share responsibility on any of the accounts, your current balance, payment history, credit limit and if the account is currently past due. Typically, positive and negative accounts will be grouped together.

If you have accounts that are negatively affecting your credit, it is important to keep in mind that you can dispute any of these issues with the credit reporting company. Barring that they will fall off your report after the issue has been resolved for seven years.

Each of your accounts can be classified in the following ways: if any of your accounts are listed as charged off, that means that the account has been written off from the creditor as a loss. While this means you may not have to pay off the account, it will still show up on your credit report for seven years. A revolving account is the classification given to credit cards, you don't need to pay these in full each month and can instead revolve them and just pay the interest.

An installment account is the classification given to loans or other accounts that involved fixed payments. An open account is the classification given to accounts that force you to pay the total balance off each month. A collection account is the classification given to any account that has been transferred to a debt collection agency, this will even show on accounts that you have settled the debt for in the past seven years.

Credit inquiries: This section of your credit report includes a list of every agency that has reviewed your credit report in the past seven years. There are two different types of inquiries, hard inquiries are made by lenders when you apply for a line of credit, too many of these in a seven-year period can negatively impact your credit score. Soft inquiries are made by you or agencies that preapprove you for lines of credit.

Credit report codes: The following is a list of codes you may see on your credit report and what they mean.

- CURR ACCT: This means the account is in good standing and current.
- CUR WAS 30-2: This means the account is currently in good standing but has been late by 30 days or more at least twice.
- PAID: This means the account is currently inactive and has been paid off
- CHARGOFF: This means the account has been charged off.
- COLLECT: This means the account has been sent to collections.
- BKLIQREQ: This means the debt has been forgiven due to bankruptcy.
- DELINQ 60: This means the account is at least 60 days past due.

CHAPTER 3

WHY YOU NEED GOOD CREDIT TODAY

These days, society is increasingly dependent on credit scores when it comes to making a wide variety of different decisions about your future. As such, if your credit isn't as good as you might like, it will affect more than just your rates on a loan or if you are eligible for a credit card. Your credit is essentially a history that shows how strict you have been when it comes to reliably paying bills on time in the past which means a wide variety of different individuals are going to be curious about it as a way of determining how you are likely to act in the future.

Your credit score can vacillate from 350, indicating you are an extremely high-risk investment, to 850, which indicates anyone who loans you money is almost certain to get it back. Additionally, your credit rating is typically shown via a numerical rating from 1 (very bad) to 9 (very good). Currently only about five percent of Americans have a credit rating of 500 or lower while about fifteen percent have a score above 800 with the majority falling between the 700 and 800 range.

Living arrangements: First and foremost, your credit score affects your ability to get a mortgage and what you will pay monthly and overall. A poor credit rating can also prevent you from successfully getting a mortgage at all, or even prevent landlords from renting to you as well. This is due to the fact that many landlords consider a lease a type of loan, after all, they are loaning you're a place to live in exchange for rent each month. If you have a low credit rating, and they do decide to rent to you, be prepared to pay extra for the privilege of having a roof over your head.

Car payments: The quality of your credit will also affect whether you will be approved for a loan for the car you are interested in purchasing as well as what your interest rate is going to be. In this case, bad credit can limit your options as fewer lenders will be willing to work with you and those that do are generally going to charge more to balance out the risk you represent. This typically translates into repayments for longer periods of time (72 months as opposed to 60 or less) and higher overall payments each month.

Job search: While the first two scenarios are to be expected, many people will be surprised to learn that a low credit score can affect your employment prospects as well. While employers can't check credit scores, they can check credit reports and many do so as a routine part of the hiring process. Depending on the job, if you have a history of poor financial responsibility an employer may be hesitant to offer you the position you have been dreaming about. Likewise, when it comes to promotions, many companies check credit reports to ensure their executives won't give the company a bad name.

Starting a business: Those who are grinding away at a 9-to-5 aren't the only ones who need to worry about their credit score, if you are self-employed a negative credit score can have even more serious implications. If you are looking to start a business with a small business loan, then you can bet lenders will check your credit score and, as most new businesses tend to fail, they will be very selective about who they lend their money to.

Monthly bills: Your credit score will also have an effect on many of your monthly bills including your utilities. Utility companies loan you their services every month and if your credit report shows that you are a risky investment then they will most definitely charge you more for the privilege of having electricity, running water, cellular service or cable and internet.

CHAPTER 4

HOW TO GET YOUR CREDIT REPORTS FOR FREE ONLINE

Every single American citizen is entitled to one free copy of each of their credit reports every twelve months. The Fair Credit Reporting Act (FCRA) means that TransUnion, Experian and Equifax are obligated to provide you with these details, but only if you ask for them. The FCRA promotes the privacy and accuracy of the information from these credit reporting agencies and is enforced by the Federal Trade Commission.

To order your free reports, all you have to do is visit AnnualCreditReport.com, fill out an Annual Credit Request Form (available at Consumer.FTC.gov) and mail it to Annual Credit Report Request Service, P.O. Box 105281, Atlanta, GA 30348-5281 or call 1-877-322-8228.

Assuming you visit the website, you will be sent to a form page where you will be required to include pertinent identifying information including your date of birth, social security number, address and name. If you have moved within the previous two years you will likely need to provide your previous address as well. Once you submit these details you will then be taken to a page that will allow you to select the reports you wish to receive, you can choose to get all three at once or to get them one at a time, it doesn't matter as long as you haven't received them in the previous 12 months.

You will then be taken to a page that will further help to verify your identity. You will receive a list of questions about the terms of your loans, your current creditors, and the like, that only you are likely to know. You will need to answer all the questions correctly which means you may need to have your current bill and loan statements handy.

There are pros and cons to pulling all three reports at once or waiting and spacing them out. If you decide to get your reports one at a time then you can space them out throughout the year, one every four months, so that you will always be aware when something new affects your credit, negatively or positively. The downside is that if there is something negative on one of your credit reports and not the others, then you will have to wait a full year to find out about it.

On the other hand, pulling all three of your credit reports at the same time will allow you to pinpoint any issues right away which means you can start working toward a solution for them as soon as possible. Additionally, this method will allow you to determine what the differences between the various reports are and if there are any discrepancies that can be easily resolved such as one of them not showing that you have finished paying off a loan. The downside is, of course, that if something happens to your credit in the next eleven months you won't know about it until the time comes to pull all three again. To mitigate this fact, you can sign up with a credit monitoring service, which will keep tabs on your credit for you in between the periods where you are eligible for a free copy of your various reports.

Be aware of imposters

While AnnualCreditReport.com is the only legitimate way to pull your credit reports on a regular basis for free, that doesn't mean it is the only site out there offering this service. While these other sites might have offers for free services, they likely come with strings attached, at best, or are simply scams designed to steal your personal information, at worst. Especially be aware of sites whose URLs are misspellings of AnnualCreditReport.com as it is unlikely that they have anything remotely close to benign intentions in mind.

Additionally, you are going to want to keep in mind that AnnualCreditReport.com verifies all of your information directly on the site which means that if you receive an email claiming to be from this site then it is likely a form of phishing that is trying to steal your personal information. Likewise, the three major credit reporting agencies never contact individuals directly which means if you receive a phone call or email from someone claiming to be with either TransUnion, Experian or Equifax then the safest choice is just to ignore it.

CHAPTER 5

WHAT AFFECTS YOUR SCORE THE MOST

There are six factors that have the most bearing on your credit score which means it will behoove you to keep an eye on all of them if you hope to retain a score as close to 850 as possible.

Credit card utilization: Your credit card utilization rate is how much credit you have available compared to how much you are currently using at any one time. It can be determined by simply dividing your credit card balances by the total limits of all of your credit cards. As such, it is beneficial to apply for a number of credit cards, even if you don't ever intend on using them. It is important to keep in mind that this amount is not calculated based on the balance that is on any one card which means you don't need to worry about maintaining a balance and rolling it over from month to month. It is always a better idea to pay off any credit card purchases as the end of the month instead.

On-time payments: Paying your bills on time is one of the easiest ways to ensure you maintain a healthy credit rating. It is weighted very heavily when it comes to influencing your credit card score which means that if you miss a few payments your score is very likely to suffer as a result.

Derogatory marks: Derogatory marks on your credit score include liens, foreclosures, bankruptcies and accounts that are in collections. Each of these will affect your credit rating significantly, with bankruptcies and foreclosures being the most serious. Derogatory marks will stay on your record for up to ten years and, assuming they are accurate, there is little you can do about removing them early. The average amount a derogatory mark will decrease your credit is 50 points.

The monetary amount that leads to the derogatory mark doesn't matter when it comes to your credit rating which means that have a single dollar sent to collections will still ding your credit 50 points. The date of the derogatory mark does matter, however, and it is based on when the negative action took place, not when it occurred. For example, if you defaulted on a debt in 2012 but the account wasn't sent to collections until 2017 then it will be listed as a recent derogatory mark and the seven-year timeframe will start in 2017, not 2012. Additionally, it is important to keep in mind that the derogatory mark will stay on your record regardless of whether or not you have since paid off the outstanding lien or collection amount.

Credit line age: The average age of your lines of credit simply refers to how long you have been building credit for. Lenders like to see that you have a long history of successfully managing credit as it makes it easier to determine if you are a risky investment or not. The longer your credit history, the more likely it is that you have been able to successfully manage your credit. As such, it is never a good idea to close out old credit card accounts, even if you don't use them anymore. Not only will this decrease your total amount of available credit, it will shrink your credit line age average as well. This doesn't just apply to credit cards but also to personal loans, student loans, auto loans and mortgages as well.

Number of accounts: As a general rule, the more lines of credit you have, the higher your credit score will be as it shows you have been given credit by more lenders. Ideally you will want to have a mix of installment and revolving credit lines for the best results. This doesn't mean you will want to go out and open as many credit cards as possible, however, as this factor weighs less heavily on your score than most.

Number of hard credit inquiries: Each time a lender checks your credit score for things like a mortgage, credit card, personal or business loan, student loan or auto loan, it will negatively affect your credit score by a few points. This effect typically wears off after a few months as long as you don't make a habit of promoting these types of checks. The effect is cumulative, however, and having multiple hard credit inquiries in a short period of time is not recommended.

CHAPTER 6

YOU HAVE AN UNFAIR ADVANATAGE WITH THE CONSUMER LAWS – USE THEM

The Fair Credit Acts

When you are going about trying to fix your credit, it can often feel as though the deck is stacked against you, however, the truth of the matter is that there are several laws that can help you to even the odds when it comes to dealing with both creditors and credit bureaus.

FCRA: The FCRA does more than just provide you with a free credit report each year, it also regulates the various credit reporting organizations and helps to ensure that the information they gather on you is both accurate and fair. This means that if you see inaccurate information on your credit report, and report it to the relevant agency, they are legally required to look into the matter and resolve it, typically within 30 days. The same applies to agencies or organizations that generally add details to your credit report. Finally, if an organization that reviews your credit report decides to charge your more or declines to do business with you based on what they find in your report, they are legally obligated to let you know why and what report they found the negative information in.

While this won't help you with that particular lender, if the information is inaccurate you will at least know where to go to clear up the issue. Additionally, if you report an inaccuracy and the credit reporting agency ignores your request you can sue them to recover the damages or a minimum of $2,500. You may also be able to win an additional amount based on punitive damages and legal fees and any other associated costs. You must file legal proceedings within 5 years of when this occurs.

Fair Credit Billing Act: This federal law is part of what is known as the Truth in Lending Act. Its purpose is to provide safeguards to consumers when it comes to unfair billing and make it clear how any errors must be corrected. This law is useful if you are charged for things you didn't purchase, are charged an inaccurate amount for products or services, you didn't receive and item you paid for, payments made aren't reflected in amounts owed or if your statements are sent to an inaccurate address.

To take advantage of this law, the first thing you need to do is to send a physical letter to the billing inquiries address that the creditor provides. You need to ensure the creditor receives your letter within 60 days from the date the error shows up on your statement. Some creditors allow for disputes to be handled online but utilizing this option can nullify your rights through this law so it is not recommended. The creditor will then have 30 days to acknowledge they received your letter and 90 days to either correct the mistake or tell you why they think it is valid. If they turn down your request you are then allowed to ask for all the documentation saying why they turned you down.

A subset of this law is what is known as the Hidden Gem Law, this means you can dispute any transaction made within 100 miles of your home, or anywhere in your home state, which exceeds $50. As long as you make a good faith effort to dispute the transaction, and return the item or stop using the service, then the company will likely refund the transaction.

Fair Debt Collection Practices Act: This is another law that benefits consumers when it comes to debt collector actions. This includes not only debt collection agencies but also their attorneys. This law prevents debt collection agencies from contacting you if you have requested that the debt be validated, contacting you instead of your attorney (if applicable) calling before 8 am or after 9 pm, contacting you at work, calling constantly, reporting false information to credit bureaus, embarrassing you in an effort to collect the debt, adding your name to a list of debtors, threatening legal action they can't actually follow through on, misrepresentation or contacting you after you have sent a letter requesting that they stop or saying that you will not pay the debt in question.

If the debt collector breaks these rules or acts in other ways they are not allowed then you can file a private lawsuit and be recouped costs, fees and damages. What's more, you don't even need to prove damages and you may be awarded a minimum of $1,000.

CHAPTER 7

HOW THE FAIR CREDIT ACTS PROTECT YOU

The FCRA is a complicated law that bears looking into a little more deeply. Likewise, just because it protects you in a wide variety of ways doesn't mean the credit reporting agency or creditors are always going to follow it the way they should. What follows are several common ways the FCRA is violated on a regular basis. If you feel as though your rights have been violated in any of these ways refer to the previous chapter.

Reporting or furnishing old information: While credit bureaus and creditors are required to keep your details as up to date as possible, you will frequently find that they fail to do so in several key ways. They will frequently fail to report that a given debt was discharged because bankruptcy was filed, that an old debt is either re-engaged or completely new, report that a closed account is active when it has actually been closed or keep information that is older than seven years (ten for bankruptcies) on your credit report. If you report these errors they are legally required to look into them within 30 days.

Reporting blatantly inaccurate information: Creditors are not allowed to provide information to credit bureaus that they know, or should know, is inaccurate. This includes classifying a debt as charged off when it was really paid in full, altering balances due, reporting a timely payment as late, listing you as the debtor when you were only an authorized user on a specific account and failing to mention when identity fraud was suspected or confirmed for a given account. Again, if you report these errors they are legally required to look into them.

Mixing up files: While it may seem surprising, credit reporting agencies frequently mix up files on individuals, potentially harming your credit score for someone else's mistakes. These issues can arise between individuals who have similar social security numbers, if you are a Junior or a Senior and the issue is with the other person's credit, mixing up details when names are similar or even mixing up details for two people with the same zip code.

Violations of debt dispute with credit reporting agencies: As previously discussed, credit reporting agencies have to follow strict rules when it comes to handling disputes; nevertheless, there are frequently issues with the ways they follow through on the process. This includes failing to notify you that a dispute has been received, failing to conduct an investigation into the dispute in a timely fashion and failing to correct disputes in a timely fashion.

Creditor debt dispute violations: The FCRA also has strict rules when it comes to how creditors must handle disputes, which are frequently disregarded. These violations include things like not notifying credit reporting agencies that a debt is being disputed, not submitting corrected information after the debt has been successfully disputed, not conducting internal investigations into the dispute once they have been notified of the error, making it difficult to submit disputes and not informing you of the results of the investigation into the dispute within five days after it has been completed.

Inaccurate credit report requests: Just because certain individuals are allowed to see your credit report doesn't mean they are allowed to do so at all times. The FCRA ensures that your credit report can't be accessed in order to determine if you are worth filing a lawsuit against, can't be accessed by employers without express permission, and can't be accessed by previous creditors related to debts that have been discharged for bankruptcy just to see what your current financial activity is.

CHAPTER 8

BOOST YOUR SCORE IN 1 DAY BY OPTING OUT AT THIS WEBSITE

OptOutPrescreen.com is a website that can allow you to opt out of offers from insurers and creditors that come in the mail offering to "preapprove" you for this or that. Taking advantage of this site to opt out of these offers will, in turn, prevent credit reporting agencies from providing your information to these companies. On this site, you can choose to opt out for five years, opt out permanently or opt back in if you change your mind. Be aware that this will only stop you from being subject to soft-credit inquiries which do not affect your credit score nearly as much (if at all) as hard credit inquiries.

You can opt out electronically for five years or permanently opt out by sending in your details in the mail. If you decide to opt out electronically you will need to provide your name, social security number, date of birth, current address and telephone number. If you decide to opt out permanently you will need to enter the same information online before being provided with a form to print off and mail.

Opting out can usually increase your score 2-7 points overnight.

CHAPTER 9

HOW TO REMOVE CREDIT INQUIRIES FAST

The Basics

Hard credit inquiries will automatically be removed from your credit report after two years. If you don't want to wait that long, you can take the following steps to remove them in a more timely fashion.

Step 1: The first thing you are going to want to do is to order your credit reports and check the inquiry section, which is generally near the bottom of the report. It is important to remember that soft inquiries, such as those that will lead you to be preapproved for offers or services will not affect your credit rating in most cases. As such you are going to want to focus on those inquiries by organizations that will actually grant you credit instead. You will ideally recognize the names of these organizations, but now and then you might come across those that are a mystery to you as well.

Step 2: Once you know what you are looking for, the next thing you are going to want to do is to find the address of each of the creditors. This information will be listed on an Experian credit report but not on Equifax or TransUnion. If the creditor doesn't show up on the Experian credit report but they do show up on the others the easiest way to get the address of the creditor is to call the credit bureau and ask for it. It is unlikely you will be able to get in touch with a live person from TransUnion, though Equifax lists an 800 number on all of their reports.

Step 3: Once you have the address in hand, the next thing you will need to do is prepare a letter asking each creditor to remove their inquiry. The FCRA ensures that only authorized inquiries will show up on your credit report which means in order to get them removed you need to challenge whether the creditor in question has authorization to pull your details. You should also send a letter to the credit bureau in question and ask that they remove the inquiry. The sample letter is below:

Date

Name
Address

(Credit Bureau Name/Creditor Name)
Address
Re: Unauthorized Credit Request

Dear (Credit Bureau Name/Creditor Name),

I recently received my (credit bureau name) credit report and I saw there was a credit inquiry from (Creditor Name) that I believe is unauthorized. I did not authorize this credit inquiry prior to it taking place which means it should not show up on my credit history. I am writing this letter to ask that you remove it from my file, as well as instigate an investigation into (Creditor Name) to determine the details behind this inquiry. When this inquiry has been completed I ask that you take the necessary steps to remove it from my file ASAP. Furthermore, I ask that you send me the documentation that will let me know that this inquiry has been removed. If you find that this inquiry was authorized, I ask that you send me proof of the authorization as well.

Thank you for your time

(Signature)

(Include credit report in question)

Step 4: Sometimes the credit bureau or creditor will just remove the inquiry without doing a full inquiry, which should be your goal. Other times they will do their due diligence and return to you the documentation that you signed giving the creditor access to your credit report. When you receive this documentation, it is important that you read it over carefully and look for any ambiguity in the wording, possibly even taking it to a lawyer depending on how badly you want the inquiry removed.

If you find some wiggle room, be sure to write back to the bureau and argue your case. Alternately, you may argue that the form was too difficult for the layman to understand. You can also threaten to contact the Banking Commission and file a complaint about the authorization form if it is not removed from your report.

Creditors will frequently ignore these requests which is why it is important to send every letter via Certified Mail and keep any receipts you receive. **If the creditor does not respond in 30 days you can then call and demand action or take legal action as described in chapter 6. If they don't respond, whether or not you authorized the inquiry becomes functionally irrelevant because they have not responded to the dispute.** Always hold you ground and demand that the inquiry be removed ASAP and make it clear that you will take the issue to the authorities if they do not comply. Keep in mind that every inquiry you have removed early will increase your credit score by several points.

Secret Inquiry Removal Strategies

Mail Certified Letters to the Creditor

This is the most effective strategy as the Creditor is the one actually reporting the negative information or responsible for the credit inquiry on your report.

Mail Certified Letters to the Repositories (Credit Bureaus)

This is not as effective anymore because the bureau will just send you a letter back that it is up to the Creditor to delete or remove inquiries. By law you can request the credit Bureau do an investigation but all they generally do is call the Creditor and verify if the inquiry was made.

Make sure you reference the Fair Credit Reporting Acts in the letters and state that the inquiry in question is invalid, unauthorized and you want it deleted immediately.

Both creditor and credit bureau only have 30 days to respond to your dispute, if they do not respond within the 30 day limit, they have to remove the inquiry by law; however, some states have recently changed this law and removed the 30 day requirement for Bureau and Creditor, unfortunately. Please be sure to check your States laws regarding the 30 day limit (a Google search will work)

When I was removing my credit inquiries, 2 out of 12 did not respond in the 30 day limit, and they were Credit bureaus not creditor, so I sent them the certified mail return receipts and proof and they had no choice but to remove the inquiries.

Why Send Certified Mail?

Because you will stand out and get attention, hardly anyone send postal mail anymore. When removed over a dozen inquiries in a month, I used certified USPS mail and I send letters to the Credit Bureaus, creditor and creditor company OWNER, which can be found by doing some research into online corporate records.

Here is a little secret most people don't know – Creditors almost always break the Fair Credit Acts because they are so vast and complex, it is nearly impossible to adhere to all of the Acts, and most court actions end in favor of the Debtor, if the Debtor challenges them, shows up and uses the Consumer laws to their rightful advantage.

If you are persistent and push your claim, you have a high chance of succeeding. But, most people DO NOT do this or they hire a credit agency to do it for them for a large ridiculous fee, and the agency doesn't do it correctly, how can they when they have 100 other people who need credit repair as well.

CHAPTER 10

HOW TO REMOVE NEGATIVE ITEMS FAST

While most issues will be removed from your credit report in seven years, (ten for bankruptcies) you may not have to wait that long if you do your due diligence. It doesn't matter if it is a foreclosure, charge off, bill in collections or late payments, they all have the potential to be removed early.

Check for errors: Studies show that more than fifty percent of all credit reports contain errors of some kind. These errors might not be major, such as including details from someone else's report, they may be smaller, and thus easier to miss. This means you are going to want to check the specifics of every entry and ensure it matches up with your personal records. You are going to want to check every credit limit, balance, payment status, account status, open and close date and account number and note any errors.

Once the errors are noted, you will then want to send a letter to each credit bureau outlining the mistakes and requesting that they are removed. You can use the letter outlined in the previous chapter and substitute in the errors you have found for the part about credit inquiries. The good part about this is that if the bureau can't determine the accuracy of the information it will simply be removed.

Goodwill letter: If you can't find any inaccuracies, or the bureau verified the ones you pointed out as correct, you can instead try sending what is known as a goodwill letter. You will send this letter to the collection agency or to the creditor and ask that they remove the negative entry based on goodwill. This will be most effective if you are looking to have charge offs, collections or late payments removed. In this letter, you will want to explain your situation to the agency in question and ask that they essentially help you out by removing the offending information. While this may seem like a long shot, it works a surprising amount of the time, especially with regards to late payments. This method is especially effective if you are a current customer and the organization has a reason to want to hold on to your business. A sample goodwill letter is below:

Date

(Creditor/Collection Agency Name)
(Creditor/Collection Agency Address)

Re: Account number provided

To whom it may concern:

I am writing regarding an issue I recently came across in my credit report (list specifics) that I was hoping you could help me to rectify. I understand that making payments on time is very important and that failing to do so causes issues for your company. If you look at my file you will see that I have done so a majority of the time I have been a client of your company and that my (late/missing) payment is an exception, not a rule. I missed the payment in question do to an (unavoidable emergency real or imagined, the more detail the better) and while I tried to make the payment on time I was unable to do so.

I can guarantee that the issue won't happen again as my (financial, physical, emotional) state has improved dramatically since (issue) and it is no longer a factor when it comes to making payments. As a courtesy, I am requesting that you make this goodwill adjustment to my record in light of my history of on time payments. This will allow me to improve my credit score and boost my confidence in being a (company name) customer.

I appreciate your time
(Signature)

Pay for delete: If you are dealing with charge offs or unpaid collections, the most effective way to have them removed from your account is to negotiate with the creditor directly and offer to pay a portion of what you owe in exchange for having the negative entry DELETED from your report. If you go down this path it is important that you get the agreement in writing prior to making the payment as once the payment is made you lose all of your leverage. A sample letter outlining this process can be found below.

Date

Collection Agency/Creditor Name
Account number:
Amount owed:

To whom it may concern,

I am writing to you in reference to the above account number in an effort to settle the amount due in a way that will benefit us both. This letter should not be seen as an acknowledgement of liability to the debt in question and I shall still retain the right to request verification of the debt from your company if the terms outlined below aren't acceptable to you. With that being said, however, I am willing to pay off (percentage of amount) of the debt as a sign of good faith based on the following conditions:

- Your company will put forth the effort to successfully remove all references to this issue from the (credit bureaus that list the issue).

- Moving forward your company will not list the debt as a settled account.

- The payment made will be consider payment in full of the debt in question.

- The debt will not be transferred or sold to a different creditor.

- This agreement will not be made public in any way, shape or form.

In exchange for these written assurances I will pay (amount about fifty percent for new accounts and thirty percent for older accounts) as soon as I receive an appropriate response. This should not be taken as a promise to pay, rather it is a restricted settlement offer based solely on your agreement to the terms outlined above. Prior to making any payments I will need a written acceptance of these terms on your company letterhead that is signed by an authorized representative of your company.

This offer will expire in 30 days, I look forward to a prompt response.

Regards,
(Typed Name)

Secret Removal Strategies

Not recommended for the reader – seek legal advice

I once had 3 credit cards that were charged off and unpaid. I sent strong letters to the credit card company and they agreed to settle but not delete the accounts.

I wanted them deleted.

I decided to look into filing a federal lawsuit pro se. I reasoned that if I can show them how serious I was and that my basis was provable in court (Credit Billing Act violations), then they would yield to my demand.

I did some research and discovered that I could file a claim in the nearest US court under Federal Question, since the Fair Credit acts are under the federal; jurisdiction. I typed up my own docket using previous cases as a template, mailed it to the Credit Card Company and credit bureaus and demanded damages of $1,000,000.

At the time I had NO CLUE what I was doing but it worked; I was so inexperienced that instead of actually filing the claim, I simply sent it to the credit card company's legal department and the credit bureau's dispute department, but with one extra step.

I also searched out the OWNER and the Statutory Agent of the credit card company by searching through the corporate records of the state they were headquartered in, and included their names in my self-created docket. **Anyone can find this information by searching for the respective states' Secretary of State Office, corporate division.**

In about 10 days I received a call from the Credit Card Company's legal firm representative. He was very calm on the phone and basically said that he tried looking my docket-case up in the Clerk online for the Ohio Northern US Court District and found nothing.

He then proceeded to state to me that he could file a suit back against my for malicious attempt, but then ended the sentence that his client wants this done and over with now, so they are prepared to delete ALL charged off credit card accounts if I agree to not sue them or follow through with the "claim"

Obviously I signed their letter stating this and in about 30 days the bureaus refreshed their data and the accounts were gone and my score **INCREASED 202 Points**!

My original goal was never to go to court but merely to settle before that.

I do not recommend you do extreme tactics like this unless you feel it really is justified, and even then be sure to seek legal advice. There are a lot of details that would go into this, let alone acting pro se.

Credit repair is a very personal and unique to each person, each case is different. I was willing to do extreme measures to get what I wanted so that I could get a mortgage loan at the time and buy a house.

CHAPTER 11

HOW TO DELETE PUBLIC COLLECTIONS AND JUDGMENTS

Public records that appear on your credit report include civil judgments, tax liens and bankruptcy filings.

Tax liens: the first thing you are going to want to do is to ensure that the debt has been paid in full. Next, you are going to want to go ahead and prepare to file a dispute. The federal government has a Fresh Start program that makes this process fairly straightforward. To qualify you are going to need to be current on your taxes and have received a Release of Tax Lien document. You will also need the original form that provided notice of the lien in the first place. You will then need to fill out IRS form 12277 Application for Withdrawal of Filed form 688Y, available at IRS.gov. You will then need to submit this, along with your original form and proof that you have paid off the lien to the IRS. You should then receive IRS form 10916(c) which states that the federal lien has been withdrawn. Finally, you will submit a copy of that form to the credit bureaus with a request that they remove the inaccurate information from your report.

Judgments: Having a judgement on your credit report can be nearly as harmful as having repossession or a loan default. While removing a judgement is possible, it is not as easy as removing a late payment or a credit inquiry. A judgement shows up on your credit report if a judge signs off on a statement saying that you owe a specific debt. This occurs when a lawsuit is filed against you for the purpose of collecting a debt, even if you weren't aware of the court proceedings at the time. It is important to keep in mind that just because a judgement was issued against you, that doesn't mean the other party was paid, which is a fact that you will use to your advantage.

There are two different ways to deal with a judgement once it has hit your credit report, you can have the judgement dismissed, also known as vacated, or remove the judgment from your credit report. If you take this second route you can contact the other party with the letter used to settle an outstanding debt from the previous chapter.

Dismiss a judgement: In order to have a judgement dismissed, you need to file a motion to dismiss the judgment with the court that issued the judgement in the first place. This is essentially an appeal that states the original outcome was inaccurate or unfair based on a specific number of reasons. First you will want to look through the proceedings and ensure that the person who requested the judgement in the first place went ahead and followed all the correct procedures and laws for doing so in your area. If there was mismanagement of this process, the odds are that the judge didn't know about it when the judgement was made.

In addition to following up on the judgement process, you will need to ensure that the person filing the judgement also followed proper court proceedings as you may be able to win out based on a technicality. This is especially important if you failed to show up for your court date and the plaintiff won by default as long as you had a valid reason for not showing up for the hearing in the first place. Again, it is important to familiarize yourself with local laws for this process to be effective.

When you prepare your motion to vacate it is important you follow local rules for civil procedure to the letter, the rules for your area should spell out exactly what you need to do, explain valid reasons a judgment can be vacated and will often include specific language you will need to use to file your motion.

The document you create should explain why the judgement should be vacated, starting with the reasons why you are bringing the motion forward. You will need to state your procedural defense and explain why you missed the original hearing if that is what happened. Valid reasons include that you were not served properly, that you responded to the summons but there was no initial judgment or that you did not have time to make it to the hearing based on when you were served. There may be other valid reasons in your area as well.

You will also need to include reasons why the judgement would have been dismissed if you had been at the hearing including things like, the collection agency failed to respond to your validation request or that the debt amount exceed local usury interest limits.

Bankruptcy: Removing a bankruptcy from your credit report is the most difficult black mark to remove. While it is far from a sure thing, a general rule is that the older the bankruptcy is, the easier it is to remove. To get started you are going to want to look for errors relating to it, if there are then you are in luck. If you find errors you can go about asking the bureau to remove them in the standard way.

Regardless if the information is accurate or not, you are still going to want to ask the bureau to verify the bankruptcy as they will be unlikely to go about doing it in the right way. Assuming they come back and tell you that it has been verified by one court or another, this is almost always inaccurate as courts rarely verify bankruptcies. With this information in hand, you will want to reach out to the court that has been specified and ask them how they verify bankruptcies. You can call and ask for this information, typically from the clerk of the court. Assuming they explain that they don't verify bankruptcies you will then want to get that fact in writing.

When you receive this letter in the mail, you will then want to send it to the bureau that claimed to have verified your bankruptcy in the first place along with a letter explaining what it is and stating that, as the bankruptcy was not actually verified, you want it taken off your record as by not doing so previously, but saying that they did, they are in direct violation of the FCRA.

Deletion of Negative Public Records (Judgements)

Ever had your wages garnished?

I did – I fought – I won

I had to pay a settlement, but I got the judgement VACATED from the clerk of court and removed completely from my credit record.

Garnishments are the worst thing for your credit, you don't want this on your report, and potential employers will have a serious problem with this.

I used whatever leverage I could find and wrote a letter to the Judge that handled the case and explained in lengthy detail how it all happened, why the creditor was being too harsh and ruthless and what violations of the Fair Credit Acts I believed they committed.

The judge actually ruled in my favor for the second hearing which I could not attend due to work, but I gave my letter to the Baliff before the court date.

I still had to pay court costs but I won. I wasn't even there, and the Creditor's attorney was very upset, apparently he losing the case really made him look bad to the firms' Partners.

Public Records will require serious measures to get vacated or deleted. **Keep in mind anything is negotiable if you can find the leverage or violation within the Fair Credit Acts. Most of the time they are there, but you have to look very hard.**

In addition, getting creditors to vacate or delete a public judgement can be accomplished with settlements and negotiations while leveraging the Fair Credit Acts. Where there is a will there is a way. Do you think attorneys give up when the odds are stacked against their case? No way, they find loopholes and any leverage they can find – I would suggest you view defending your credit report the same way, only the consumer laws are MORE biased for you (in your favor).

CHAPTER 12

SECTION 609 CREDIT REPAIR METHOD

To understand how the Section 609 credit repair method works, it is important to understand that the FCRA was written before the advent of the internet. As such, they require the credit reporting agencies to have physical copies of all documentation to support each account that is being reported on. This is a problem for these agencies as virtually all credit items added to your credit report these days are submitted electronically. This, in turn, means that it is rare for any documents to be reviewed prior to changes being made to your credit report.

Essentially, the credit reporting agencies just give all creditors the benefit of the doubt when new information is added to your file. You can use this to your advantage by asking for hard-copy verification via Section 609 of the FCRA for virtually anything negative that is listed on your credit report. You simply need to use the following letter and not be deterred by any scare tactics that the credit reporting agencies will use to cover their tracks as they will try everything in their power to avoid having to tell you that they don't have the physical documentation.

With the following letter, you will need to be sure to always include a copy of a photo identification as well as a copy of your social security card(also include your past residences for 5 years). **This is due to the fact that the FCRA only requires the credit reporting agencies to respond to individuals in writing if they provide these details.** Without it, your letters will simply be ignored. When disputing accounts, it is also important to never dispute more than 22 at one time. This is the magic number, anything more than that will cause you dispute to be considered frivolous. **Additionally, you will want to ensure you hand label your envelopes as type envelopes will be opened far less often.**

Name

Address

(Credit Bureau Name)

Date

To Whom It May Concern:

This letter is a formal complaint that you are reporting inaccurate and incomplete credit information. I am distressed that you have included the below information in my credit profile and have failed to maintain reasonable procedures in your operations to assure maximum possible accuracy in the credit reports you publish.

Credit reporting laws ensure that bureaus report only 100% accurate credit information. Every step must be taken to assure the information reported is completely accurate and correct. The following information therefore needs to be re-investigated. I respectfully request to be provided proof that these inquiries were in fact authorized with an instrument bearing my signature, and for legitimate business purposes. Failing that, the unauthorized inquiry must be deleted from the report as soon as possible:

(Accounts you wish to have removed from your report)

Please delete this misleading information, and supply a corrected credit profile to all creditors who have received a copy within the last 6 months, or the last 2 years for employment purposes.

Additionally, please provide the name, address, and telephone number of each credit grantor or other subscriber.

Under federal law, you have 30 days to complete your re-investigation. Be advised that the description of the procedure used to determine the accuracy and completeness of the information is hereby requested as well, to be provided within 15 days of the completion of your re-investigation.

Sincerely,

(Signature)

Name

SSN#

CHAPTER 13

FAST CREDIT REPAIR AFTER FORECLOSURE

While rebuilding your credit after a foreclosure is difficult, it is doable if you go about it in the right way and stick to your guns in the process. It is not going to be an overnight process but slow and steady wins the race.

Credit cards: After a foreclosure, many credit card companies will contact you in an attempt to either cancel your account or to raise your rates. Despite what they may say, this is only an automatic adjustment that was triggered based on your foreclosure and is in no way a sure thing. As long as you have been paying your bill on time and are not using the credit card for major purchases, there is no reason you cannot negotiate with the representative that you speak with to both keep your card and keep your rate at the level it was at prior to the foreclosure. Be steadfast in your commitment and don't let them bully you around and you can come out on top.

It is important to keep your credit cards if at all possible as using them is a great way to start reestablishing your credit. You are going to want to use them for household expenses and to pay the charges off in full each month. Maintaining consistency and keeping a clean record of on-time payments is the first step to rebuilding credit.

Secured credit: If you have already lost your credit cards then the easiest way to go about rebuilding your credit is to start with a secured credit card. A secured credit card works like a regular credit card except your limit is tied to the amount of money you deposit with the credit card company up front. You will not be able to access that money directly while the account is open which means the lender doesn't have to worry about losing out on any credit loans that are made in your name.

A secured credit card is different than a debit card in that the company providing it to you will go ahead and make monthly reports to the credit bureaus, helping to build your credit as long as you use it in a conscientious fashion. The card also has all of the fees and penalties of a regular credit card so it is important to shop around for one offers the best rates.

Avoid new debt: When rebuilding your credit, it is important that you don't take on any new debt until your credit score has started to right itself as your debt to income ratio will affect your credit score and, at the moment, you will need all the help you can get. Likewise, starting several new credit streams at once will only shorten the average length of your credit history which can send you back in the other direction. Rather than open new avenues for credit, and debt, focus on paying off any other debts you may current have and save money for when you score gets above 650 so that you can take on new debt with better rates.

Try Low Balance Credit Credits: These credit cards usually have extremely high interest rates but your goal is to charge only 10% of the balance to build a credit score fast. Getting 3-4 of these can achieve excellent results fast if you charge and keep a low (10%) balances on them with no changes. I still have some of my low balance cards that I got just for the purpose of credit repair years ago. For instance I have a $2,000 and $1,000 card. On the $1,000 card I hold a balance of $155 and on the $2,000 card I keep a balance of $180.

Consider credit unions: A credit union is essentially a nonprofit bank that operates only to benefit its members. As such, when you are ready to apply for a new loan or a credit card it is recommended that you join a credit union to do so as the rates that you are eligible for are going to typically be much more in your favor than through a traditional bank. They will also be more likely to overlook your financial mishap as their requirements for loans and credit cards won't be as strict as well.

CHAPTER 14

FAST CREDIT REPAIR AFTER MEDICAL JUDGMENTS

Unexpected medical expenses can sneak up on anyone at any time with no warning. If a medical judgement is issued against you for costs associated with this type of scenario, the first thing you are going to want to do is to try and fight it using the tactics discussed in chapter 11. If that doesn't work, however, then you are going to have a black mark on your credit report for the next seven years. The most important thing to do in this instance is to not lose hope and to instead do everything you can to repair your credit as quickly as possible.

Negotiate your debt: As previously noted, just because a judgement is filed against you doesn't mean the plaintiff is going to get paid. Medical establishments are aware of this fact which means you can likely negotiate a more reasonable fee as opposed to simply paying what a judge says you owe.

In order to do this, the first thing you are going to need to do is to organize and review your medical bills to ensure they are free of errors including double charges or overcharges. Billing items you can contest include things like full-day charges for the day you were released from the hospital, medication charges and secondary charges for standard supplies such as sheets and gowns as these should be factored into the daily fees. Additionally, if you have insurance you should see a deduction for what they paid on your bill as well.

Once you know exactly what you have to pay, you will then want to compare that amount to your monthly bills and determine how much you can afford to pay of the bill in question. If you only have a small percentage of the total available currently, the best bet is to wait until you have at least fifty percent of the total saved and then reach out to the plaintiff and offer to settle. You can either call the other party or send out the pay for delete letter from chapter 10. Regardless, if you come to an agreement make sure you get it in writing.

Play catchup: If you spent time recuperating from a major illness or accident then it is likely that your medical expenses aren't the only thing you have to deal with, which means the first step to rebuilding your credit is to get your other payments back on track. To do so, you are going to want to contact each of your creditors and explain the situation and ask if you can work out some type of payment plan to get back on track. Generally, you will be able to come to an agreement that you can both live with that won't leave you completely broke. Getting back into the habit of paying all of your bills on time is a crucial step towards rebuilding your credit.

Installment accounts: In addition to opening a secured credit card as described in the previous chapter, you are going to want to go about building positive credit by obtaining an installment loan.

This is a loan for a set amount with a set term and a set repayment. Installment loans are easier to get that rotating loans (such as standard credit cards) as the risk to the lender is lessened.

Even still, depending on your current level of credit you may need to get someone who trusts you to cosign on the loan. A cosigner is someone with good credit who essentially gives their word that you are going to pay back the loan, otherwise the failure hurts their credit as well. A good place to look for a starter installment loan is from an independent automotive dealership. These dealers are going to have less stringent requirements than major chains and are often more accustomed to dealing with individuals with less than stellar credit. You may not even need a cosigner after all. If you do get a loan in this fashion, make it a point of always paying the bill on time as this fact will be reported to the credit bureaus on a monthly basis.

CHAPTER 15

QUICK TECHNIQUES TO REBUILD CREDIT

Pay off what you owe: While this is going to be easier said than done in most situations, according to Experian, the ideal amount of credit utilization that you want is 30 percent or less. While there are other ways to increase your credit utilization rating, paying off what you owe on time each month will also go towards showing you can pay your bills on time, essentially pulling double duty when it comes to improving your credit score. It will also make it easier to follow through on the following tips.

Pay your credit card bills twice a month: If you have a credit card that you use on a regular basis, say for example because it offers you reward points, so much so that you max it out each month, it may actually be hurting your credit even though you pay it off in full at the end of each month. This may be the case due to the way the credit card company reports to the credit bureau; depending on when they report each month it could show that your credit utilization rate is close to 100 percent depending on what your credit line currently is, thus hurting your credit score. As such, paying off your credit card in two smaller chunks throughout the month can actually help boost your credit without costing you anything extra overall.

Increase your credit limit: If you aren't currently in a position to pay down your credit card balance, you can still improve your credit utilization rate by increasing your current credit limit. This is an easy way to improve your credit utilization rate without putting any more money out up front. If you do this, however, it is important that you don't take advantage of the increased credit line as if you find yourself up against the limit again you will be worse off than when you started. Only pursue this option if you have the willpower to avoid racking up extra charges, especially if you are already strapped when it comes to the payments you need to make each month; decreasing your credit utilization limit while also making more late payments is a lateral move at best.

Open a new account: Improving your credit utilization rate is one of the best ways to start rebuilding your credit. If your current credit card company won't increase your credit limit you may way to try applying for another credit card instead. If your credit is not so hot then your rates are going to be higher, but this won't matter as long as you don't plan on using the card in the first place. Remember, credit utilization rate is a combination of your total available lines of credit so this can be a good way to drop your current utilization rate substantially, especially if you won't be able to pay off what you currently owe for a significant period of time.

Keep in mind, however, that if you choose this route then you are only going to want to apply for one new card every couple of months, especially if you aren't sure if you are going to be approved, as too many hard credit inquiries will only cause your credit score to drop, even if you do end up with a better credit utilization rate as a result. Spreading out these requests will give the inquiries time to drop off naturally and will prevent you from looking desperate to potential lenders which can also make it more difficult to get a new card.

Authorized users: If you don't have the credit to get a new credit card, or even to extend your current credit line, then your best choice may be to find someone you trust and ask them to become an authorized user on their card. While most people will likely balk at the idea, you may be able to pacify them by explaining that you don't need a copy of their card or have any intent on using it, simply being listed on the card is enough to improve your credit utilization rating. Not only that, but you will also get credit for the on-time payments that this other person makes as well.

CHAPTER 16

HOW TO GET LENDER OFFERS

A vast majority of lenders don't have offers that are clearly defined up front, instead they have a general loan package that can be tweaked based on the situation individuals who come to them find themselves in. With this in mind, it becomes apparent why it is so important to seek out multiple offers before making a decision.

Depending on your FICO score, lenders may be more than happy to compete for your business. This fact, coupled with the lack of predetermined rates means that you can easily improve your results by shopping around and then singling out lenders who almost have the rates you are looking for and then telling them that you can get a better deal elsewhere.

To maximize this strategy, you are going to want to make a list of the features you are absolutely going to need to be happy with a given loan and then call each lender you have already talked to and go down the list point by point. If you come across a lender who has an approach that appeals to you, let the other lenders know about it and see what they can do to either match or beat it. They know they are in a competitive business and if you are willing to force their hand they will show you just how much they want your business.

Pre-approved offers: If you took advantage of OptOutPrescreen.com to limit soft inquiries on your credit report and are planning on looking for lenders anytime soon then you may want to reconsider and opt back in, at least for the relatively near future. If you have not opted out of the system, and your credit isn't terrible, then putting in an application with one lender will likely trigger a barrage of competing offers from other lenders as creditors will happily provide your information to anyone and everyone who is interested in selling you on their services.

While this can be annoying in some cases, if you are looking for the best lender possible then it could be just what you need to pit several lenders against one another. Prescreened offers can make it easier for you to compare relative costs or special offers as long as you do your due diligence with each and ensure that you aren't being hornswoggled by smoke and mirrors.

Ensure you have a loan estimate document: The loan estimate document was created by the Consumer Financial Protection Bureau to make it easier for borrowers to compare the various costs associated with individual loans and lenders. Its job is to standardize and simplify the way that lenders expose their fees so that you aren't comparing apples to oranges. The loan estimate document can be downloaded from ConsumerFinance.gov.

In addition to make it easier to compare various potential loans, it makes it easy to be aware of the various fees that are sure to pile up along the way, even with the most apparently straightforward of loans. It also breaks down costs in a way that anyone can understand without the help of a CPA. It includes all sorts of useful information including estimated monthly payments, prepayment penalties and the interest rate of the various loans in question.

Lock in the best rate: Once you have done the work of comparing the various options available to you, the next thing you are going to want to do is to ensure that the best option doesn't change while you are making all of the relevant arrangements. To ensure this is the case you are going to want to ask the lender for a written rate lock or lock-in. This is a written and legally binding guarantee that the lender will give you the interest rate you discussed for the price you discussed for a set period of time. It protects you from interest rate increases that may occur while your loan is being processed. It is important to keep in mind that some lenders will charge for a lock-in while others will not it all depends on the individual lender.

CHAPTER 17

HOW TO BUILD BUSINESS CREDIT

Approximately 45 percent of all small businesses who are turned down for a loan have bad credit to blame, according to the Federal Reserve Banks of Philadelphia, Cleveland, Atlanta and New York. A robust credit profile for your business doesn't just make it easier to get a loan, it will also make it easier for your business to attract new customers. This is because, unlike with your personal credit report, anyone including potential suppliers, partners and customers can all see the credit report of your business at any time. With this fact in mind, it should be clear that if you own a small business, you will want to do everything in your power to improve its credit as quickly as possible and keep it clean as well.

Know your current score: While you are already familiar with Equifax and Experian, when it comes to keeping tabs on your business credit score you are also going to need to familiarize yourself with the Dun & Bradstreet credit bureau. Unfortunately, while determining your personal credit score is relatively straightforward, all three bureaus use a different means of determining business credit scores as well as asking various lenders for differing types of data. This will sometimes work to your advantage, however as Dun & Bradstreet lets business owners update their basic business details and also upload financial data. Even better complete portfolios actually improving overall credit scores.

Set up trade lines: Assuming you purchase materials from third-party vendors, doing so in the right way can help you to improve your business' credit. Assuming you have been working with a given vendor for some time, it is likely that they would be willing to extend you trade credit for the things you purchase most often. Trade credit simply means that you will be able to pay a predetermined number of weeks, or even just days, after you have received the latest shipment of inventory. Once you set up this type of relationship it is then easy to ask the supplier to report your payments to the relevant credit bureaus.

You will want to try your hardest to establish at least three of these types of relationships as doing so will allow you to get what is known as a Paydex score through Dun & Bradstreet which is a measure of your successful payment history. Even if you form relationships with smaller vendors who don't typically report details, by listing them on your account as trade references the bureau will then follow up with them to generate your score.

Be prompt with payments: Just like with your personal finances, paying creditors on time is a crucial part of building your business credit successfully. If you are looking to get the best Paydex score from Dun & Bradstreet you are going to need to go above and beyond and make all your payments early, no exceptions. Additionally, the longer your credit history the better so the sooner you can start forming these relationships the better it will be for your score.

Borrow from the right lenders: While having a loan and paying it on time can help to boost your business' credit score, this will only be the case if the lender you choose reports to the bureaus which is far from guaranteed. Do your homework and make sure that your fiscal responsibility is helping you out as much as possible when you do get a loan. Most banks will report to the bureaus as do the online lenders including BlueVine, Kabbage, Funding Circle Fundation, Lending Club and OnDeck. Fundbox, Lighter Captial, SmarBiz and most merchant cash advance companies do not. If you are using business credit cards, strive to keep your credit utilization under 20 percent for the best results.

Be aware of your public records: Just like your business credit report, your public records can also be seen by anyone which means you are going to want to do your best to stay on the right side the law. Not only will negative public records affect your business credit score, they will affect the way the public perceives your business as well.

CHAPTER 18

STOP COLLECTORS FAST

While it is always going to be a better choice to deal with creditors directly rather than waiting for a debt to reach collections, if it does reach this point it is important to keep in mind that you still have options thanks to what is known as the Fair Debt Collection Practices act.

Ask for details in writing: Within 5 days of making contact, a debt collector is obligated to send you a written notice outlining the amount of money you owe, who you owe it to and how to dispute the claim. Most debt collectors won't do this automatically, however which means the first contact you have with them should include asking for this information and nothing else. The goal of the debt collector is to force you to confirm that you will pay the debt or make a payment, and not having all of the details in front of you can make it easy to say the wrong thing and wave many of your rights without even realizing it. What's more, asking for a copy of the details will prevent them from contacting you again until you have received them, giving you some time to get your defenses together if you have been caught off guard.

Dispute the claim: Once you have received the details of the claim in writing, the next thing you are going to want to do is to dispute the claim using the methods discussed in previous chapters, regardless of whether or not you believe you owe the money in question. This will put the onus on the collection agency to verify the debt, which is far from a sure thing even on debts that you do owe. You have 30 days to send this letter from the date you received the details which means that using certified mail is key. Be sure to ask for a delivery receipt as nine times out of ten the collections agency will deny they received your request. Once you send this letter and notify the collection agency of this fact, they cannot contact you again until the debt has been verified. **They also have to stop all reporting activity, make sure you demand this in the letter.**

Keep track of everything: As discussed previously, debt collectors are limited in how they can approach you but, in most cases, will try and skirt these restrictions as much as possible in an effort to get you to agree to pay the debt or set up a payment plan. As such, it is in your best interest to take detailed notes every time you speak with them and keep anything they send you so you can look it over for violations at a later date.

Illegal activities not previously covered include speaking to anyone but you or your representation about the debt, using abusive language, misrepresenting the amount of the debt of making false claims about legal action, seizing property or garnishing wages if they don't intend to actually follow through. If they do any of these things, then the issue of the amount of debt you owe will essentially become moot as you will be able to take legal action against them and even the threat of doing so will often be enough for them to forgive some or all of your debt entirely. Be sure not to mention that you are keeping track of your conversations as this will cause them to be on their best behavior and decrease your potential for leverage.

Speak as little as possible: Everything that a debt collector says is for the purpose of collecting on the debt which means that the less you say, the less they have to use against you. Remember, regardless of what they may say up front, they are never really your friend, nor do they have your best interests at heart. They work on commission which means the more they get from you the more they will make. Never commit to anything, never agree that you owe the amount in question, always mention that you are considering bankruptcy and discuss payment options only if you intend to follow through. If they determine that you are unlikely to pay, and the amount owed is less than $2,500, they may give up and consider you more trouble than you are worth. While the debt will remain on your credit report for the next seven years, it might be worth it, depending on your current financial situation.

Be aware of time limits: Once you receive the details from the collection agency, you will need to look into the timeframe which they have to collect on the debt based on where you live (between three and six years in most cases). Once this period of time has passed they can no longer take legal action against you. It is important to be aware of these limits as if you make a payment after this period of time, some states will allow the clock to be reset, the same can be said for acknowledging you owe the debt or for signing up for a repayment plan.

CHAPTER 19

HOW TO NEGOTIATE AND SETTLE LARGE DEBTS

While creditors would like you to think otherwise, the fact of the matter is that any debt that you have is negotiable. What's more, regardless of the amount, 90 percent of creditors are going to be willing to take a lump sum now over a promise to pay at a later date. When it comes to negotiating large amounts, the following tips may make it easier to come out ahead.

Have a story and stick with it: The person you are dealing with isn't going to be interested in your life story, but they will need to know why you are unable to pay in full right now. This means you are going to want to have a story that outlines your hardships and explains what you are doing to get back on track. You will want to distill that story down to the most important points and never waver from it throughout the negotiation process.

One particularly useful strategy is mentioning that, due to financial hardship, you will soon be meeting with a lawyer who specializes in bankruptcy. This will almost always make creditors more willing to strike a deal as if you file for bankruptcy there is a chance that they will get nothing.

Stay calm: It is important to keep in mind that, no matter what the creditor says, you have the upper hand as the debt you have is leverage over them. Stick to this fact and, no matter what they say, do your best to avoid losing your temper. If you make a scene or cause drama then the creditor will know they are getting to you and will be less willing to make a deal. If you feel yourself losing it, simply tell them that you will call them back and end the call as quickly as possible. If you find the creditor's behavior hard to stomach, simply tell them you are recording the conversation which will put them on their best, and most professional, behavior.

Always ask questions: If the creditor threatens you with a lawsuit or with the loss of property, above all else it is important that you don't let these threats frighten you into making a poor decision. Instead, it is important to ask questions as this will often reveal if the creditor is bluffing or not. For example, if they threaten you with a lawsuit, simply ask when you can expect to be notified of it. Keep notes of these threats as they are often times illegal as creditors are strictly limited as to how they can approach debt, specifically to protect consumers.

Likewise, you are going to want to take notes every time you speak with a creditor including the name of the person you spoke with, the date and the things that were discussed, especially threats. There is typically a statute of limitations as to how long the creditor has to collect on a debt, which varies by region, and they will likely become irater as that time period approaches.

Avoid agreeing to a payment plan: If you agree to a payment plan you will always end up paying more in the long run then if you manage to scrape together a lump sum payment. Depending on the amount you owe, even as little as 30 percent might be enough to satisfy the creditor assuming it is getting close to the end of the timeframe they have to collect on the debt and you have stuck to your story about financial hardship and bankruptcy. Never be afraid to offer a lowball number, the worst that can happen is that they refuse to take it. If you do end up agreeing to a payment plan make sure you go over your expenses with a fine-tooth comb and ensure you can afford to make the payment every month to avoid finding yourself back in the same situation.

Try and deal with creditors: If you know you are going to be unable to make payments on a debt you have accrued, do your best to come to an agreement with the creditor directly, before the debt is sent to collections. The creditor is always going to be easier to negotiate with than a third-party debt collection service.

CHAPTER 20

MAINTAING YOUR CREDIT

Once you have done the work of repairing your damaged credit score you are going to want to do everything in your power in order to ensure that you don't find yourself back where you started. You have worked diligently to repair the mistakes of the past, don't use it as an excuse to start making new ones. To help keep you on the straight and narrow, consider the following tips.

Always pay your bills on time, all of them: While not every bill that you have will end up on your credit report if you are a few days late when it comes to paying it, you can never know for certain which bills are mission critical and which can be safely ignored until your next pay check. Even a small fine from the local library could ultimately end up on your credit report, dinging your hard-won credit score in the process. Don't take that chance and always remain vigilant when it comes to paying your bills on time.

Avoid using credit cards: While having credit cards improves your credit utilization and credit history, using them too often is a surefire way to start back-sliding, especially if your budget is on the lean side. If you must use your credit cards, take special care to ensure that you never exceed a credit utilization of 30 percent as that's when your credit score will start to take a hit. While going over this limit slightly will only affect your score by a few points, if you are just on the edge of an acceptable score, that might be all it takes to start seeing higher rates as a result.

Pay down your loans: Once you have righted your financial ship, the best way you can keep it on course is to make it a point of paying down your loans as quickly as possible; don't forget, approximately 30 percent of your credit score is influenced by the amount of debt you have which makes it one of the easiest ways to continue improving your score once you are moving in the right direction.

In order to make more money available to pay down your debt, the first thing you are going to want to do is to stop living paycheck to paycheck which means establishing an emergency fund. A solid emergency fund will allow you to live for three months, and pay all your bills, if the worst happens and you find yourself out of the job. Establishing this fund will give you the wiggle room you need to prioritize your debt without worrying about every minor pitfall that comes your way.

Monitor spending: Approximately 40 percent of individuals who find themselves with credit score issues got there simply by not keeping track of their week-to-week spending as well as they should. With the prevalence of online banking, there is no reason why you shouldn't be aware of exactly what your checking account balance is, every minute of every day. Get in the habit of monitoring your spending and you will never be surprised when your bank statement shows up at the end of the month. This doesn't mean you won't want to peruse the statement when it does come in, however, as you never know when a mistake might be made, you never know when a little extra diligence could pay off in a big way.

Remain glued to your credit report: Just because you are out of the woods doesn't mean that nothing new is going to show up on your credit report, whether it is your fault or not. Something new from your past might show up, or one of the bureaus may make a mistake or fail to note the positive changes you have made in a timely manner. The previous chapters have given you tools for dealing with these issues, but you will only be able to put them into action if you are aware of them in the first place. Don't let all your hard work go to waste, continue taking advantage of your free credit report every year.

CHAPTER 21

FRAUD AND IDENTITY THEFT PREVENTION

Once you have established a quality credit score, you need to do your best to protect it by taking extra steps to prevent identity theft and other types of fraud. The following tips will help you do so:

Respond to voicemail intelligently: If you receive a voicemail from someone claiming to be from your credit card company or bank, only respond by calling back the number that is printed on your card. This is the only number you can guarantee won't lead to a fraud scenario. The same goes for emails, even if they appear to be legitimate, you should only ever contact your bank or credit card company through obviously official channels that you instigate to ensure they are legitimate.

Take extra care with signatures: Not many people are aware, but you can actually sign your credit and debit cards with the phrase "see identification". While this will force you to show your ID much more frequently, it will also prevent anyone who is attempting to use it illegally from being able to do so. Unless they have a fake ID with your name and accurate signature they will be out of luck.

Be frugal with your credit card number: Ninety percent of the time any website that asks for your credit or debit card number "for identification purposes" has only dubious intentions in mind. Unless you are planning on buying something from the site you are going to want to avoid providing this information. The fewer places that your personal details are available online the less risk you run of falling victim to fraud.

Be diligent about your privacy: Even if you have already set them to the max settings, it is important to check both your browser and social media settings on a regular basis to ensure they are as you left them. You never know when an update could have come along and reset them or changed something else that affected them in some way. It only takes one slip to allow someone with malicious intent through, which is why it pays to stay vigilant. Likewise, every time you visit a secure website, take an extra moment to clear your browser's cache and history to prevent anyone from tracking down personal information that way.

Unsubscribe sparingly: If you receive an email newsletter and you aren't sure where it came from, never click the unsubscribe button. This will let the spammer know that they have a live email address and they will redouble their efforts, at best, or initiate additional tactics to procure your private data now that they have your email address, at worst. Even if the spammer has no ulterior motives than to get you to read their newsletter you are always better off just hitting the spam button and forgetting about it.

Be aware of online store security: When you are shopping online be sure to make a point of never entering sensitive information if the website isn't secure. You can determine if a site is using a secure connection if the web address starts with https or if it features a padlock icon in the top right corner. Either of these are an indicator that the website is encrypted which will make it much more difficult for fraud to occur based on the transaction. Entering your details via a standard http connection is little more than asking for trouble.

Have varying passwords: In addition to the obvious, such as not using birthdays or loved ones' names as passwords, it is important to have varying levels of password security for the most secure results. You are going to want to have at least one password for low-security sites that you aren't terribly worried about being hacked, a more secure password for online stores and the like and a separate password entirely when it comes to banks or credit card websites that are more complicated still. You should never store your passwords anywhere on your computer or anywhere in real life where other people, with potentially malicious intent, are likely to have access to and, if you must write them down, don't keep them near your computer.

Cyber Threats & Privacy

Identity theft and hacking are growing at super exponential rates. It won't stop and will only get worse. The fact is that most Americans are already compromised and they don't even know it. It is estimated that over 80% of all residential households in American do not even have their WiFi router secured properly.

Wireless Credit Card Scanners

These are hackers that will scan your credit card in your pocket at coffee shops or other unassuming public places. They have special devices or programs that can "see" the RF chips embedded in your credit card on their laptops. This happened to me once but since I was set up on **banking text alerts** I was able to stop it and get my money back. I now use radio frequency shield card slots and wallets to prevent this from happening again, which you can buy on Amazon.

Online Banking

Make sure your WIFI network is secure and the browser is set to HTTPS when logging into your banking account. One small compromise and someone can steal your info, and ruin your credit. In fact any website you submit personal information on should start with HTTPS (Secure) URL.

In addition, over 80% of all U.S. homes do not secure their wifi router. Most people never change their factory default router login and password. Any hacker that scans your neighborhood (and yes they still do this) can generally tell what kind of router model you have from the SSID default and then check to see if they can login using the default pass and user name. If a hacker is able to break into your home wireless or wired network, you can be seriously compromised. This often leads to identity fraud and theft. Most often you will not even know about it until well after it has occurred and someone has used your information to steal your money or identity.

The cyber threats are very real and much worse than you think; they are only getting more complex everyday as hackers develop new technologies to scan for weaknesses and infiltrate unassuming people and businesses.

Shred your mail, bills or paperwork that may have sensitive personal info on them. You would be surprised to know that people still rummage through garbage to find data to sell or use for gain.

Use Secured Email

Almost everyone sends sensitive info via email and text not even thinking that someone can scan that data in "cyberspace" if they are looking for it. Since most people are now using Gmail,Yahoo Hotmail, etc. There aren't very many secure options for email if you are not using Thunderbird or Outlook. However, there is one company in Switzerland that has a service call Protonmail.com.

It a browser email account with mobile phone apps that send and received encrypted mail and is very easy to use. They have a free account version and a paid account version, which is approximately $6 per month. If you send personal data via email such as tax returns, social security numbers, credit card numbers... **Check out ProtonMail.com**

Commercial Mailbox

Use a commercial mail box, such as the UPS store mail box, for receiving your postal mail instead of receiving it at home. UPS Stores are very flexible and can even forward your mail wherever you are. Many thieves still steal mail in an attempt to find social security numbers, checks, or anything they can use to extract money or credit from a victim.

CONCLUSION

Just because you've finished this book doesn't mean there is nothing left to learn on the topic, expanding your horizons is the only way to find the mastery you seek. While laws regarding these issues are fairly set in stone, the credit bureaus are always petitioning the federal government to update the FCRA to focus on electronic forms of communication which means looking up the latest rulings is always encouraged.

The next step is to stop reading already and to get ready to get started rebuilding your credit as quickly and effectively as possible. While you are certainly facing an uphill battle, it is important to keep in mind that it is far from unwinnable, and the information discussed in the preceding chapters will go a long way towards making your fight a lot more manageable. Above all, it is important to keep in mind that repairing your credit is a marathon, not a sprint which means that slow and steady wins the race. Make a plan, stick with it, and you will be able to improve your credit score by 100 points or more sooner than you may think.

If you found this book useful in anyway, a review on Amazon is always appreciated!

www.ingramcontent.com/pod-product-compliance
Lightning Source LLC
Chambersburg PA
CBHW030447220526
45464CB00006B/2439